W9-DCY-016

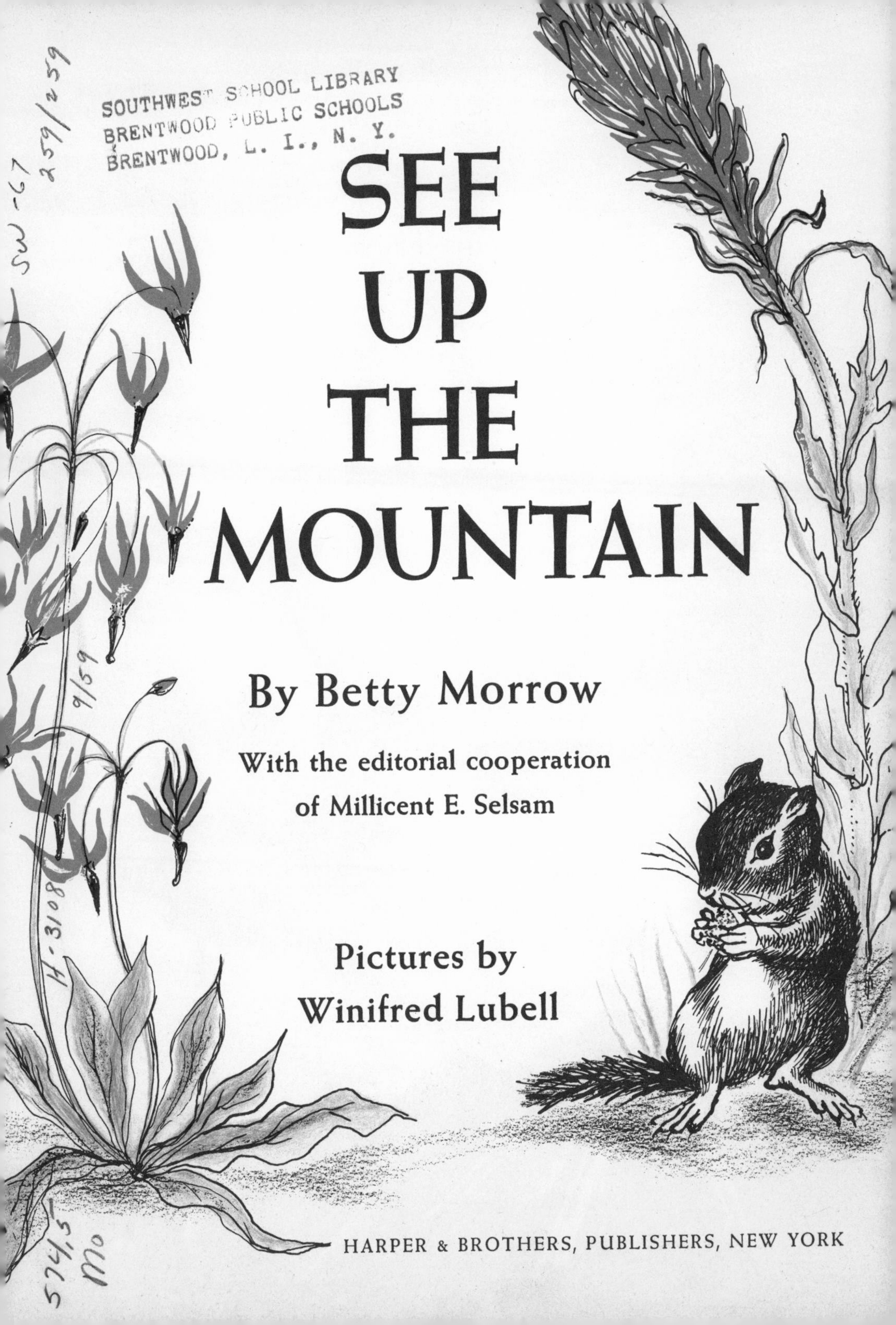

SEE UP THE MOUNTAIN

By Betty Morrow

With the editorial cooperation
of Millicent E. Selsam

Pictures by
Winifred Lubell

HARPER & BROTHERS, PUBLISHERS, NEW YORK

SEE UP THE MOUNTAIN

Printed in the United States of America

Library of Congress catalog card number: 58-7758

SEE UP THE MOUNTAIN

,000
eet
,000
eet
,50C
eet
000
eet

Here is a mountain. We are going to climb it.

We look up and see that a mountain is not the same from bottom to top. Directly above us, all the way to an altitude of 4,000 feet, we see the brown and yellow of open, hilly fields with green trees making splashes of shadow. Above that, up to about 6,500 feet, is the dark green of tall forest. From 6,500 to 9,000 feet there is still more forest green—but softer and thinner, and broken here and there by patches of bright green meadow. In the 1,000 feet above that we catch sight of gray and brown and even pink rocks, with a few spots of grayish-green trees. The very top of the mountain, above 10,000 feet, is white with snow even in midsummer.

These are the colors of the mountain. As we climb into them, we'll see that they mark off the different parts, or zones, of the mountain, just as colors mark off the different states or countries on a map.

All the way up, each part of the mountain has its own kind of soil and climate. It has its own kind of plants and animals, too. So keep your eyes open as we climb from one zone to the next. You will know some of the animals and plants right away. But others will be new to you, because they do not grow in the lowlands.

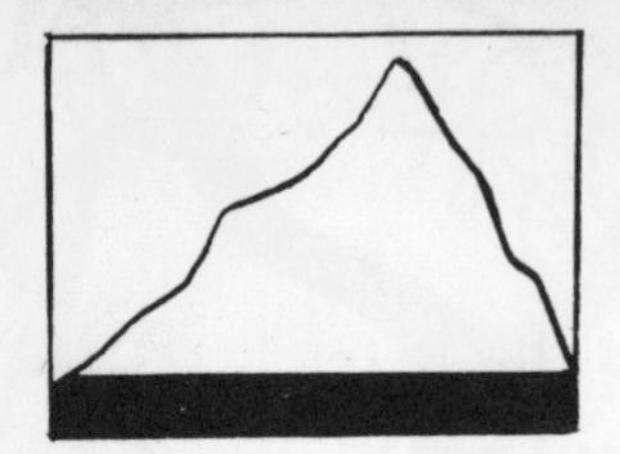

The trail is waiting. Up we go.

We are going up about 11,000 feet from the bottom of the valley—a little more than two miles straight up. But our trail will wind back and forth, so we'll walk a lot farther than that. Our feet will carry us many miles around the bends in the trail.

Just as no two trees are exactly alike, so each mountain is different from every other one. Our mountain is in California but it shows very clearly some important facts about *all* high mountains, whether they are in California or Colorado or New Hampshire, in North America or Europe or Asia.

It's hot here on the lowest part of the mountain. The sun beats down, and the grass is brown and dry. Let's rest here a minute and look around.

At first everything seems quiet but as we listen our ears catch tiny rustlings everywhere. A brown lizard comes out to sun itself. It's hard to see because it's almost the same color as the rock on which it is lying. A little striped chipmunk dashes across the trail, looking for a meal of seeds from the cones of that low digger pine. A cottontail rabbit hunches down among the manzanita bushes.

It's time to move on. Are these the only living things in this quiet place? As we walk along, we see a footprint like a tiny hand in the dust of the trail. A raccoon must have been out last night, but now it's asleep in its nest in that old hollow tree. The white-footed mice are asleep, too. We know there are thousands of them all around us, even though we don't see them in the daytime. They are safe now from the hawks, but when they come out at night to look for seeds and berries, owls will be looking for them.

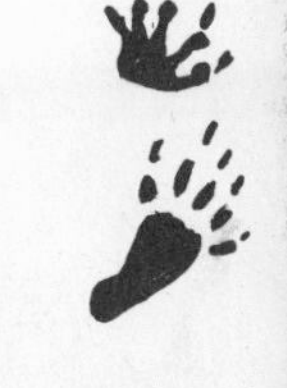

We stroll up a hillside covered with fluffy gray bushes. A high shrill call stops us in our tracks. Out from the brush marches a mother quail with her babies. The tall feather on top of her head bobs up and down as she walks along. Her brownish-gray feathers blend with the brown grass and gray bushes. She calls again, and another quail answers. We tiptoe toward the quail family—but not softly enough. Mother and babies rush back into the brush.

Don't step over that fallen log until we see what's on the other side. A rattlesnake is lying there waiting for a meal of chipmunk to come its way. If we don't disturb it, it won't disturb us, so let's go on.

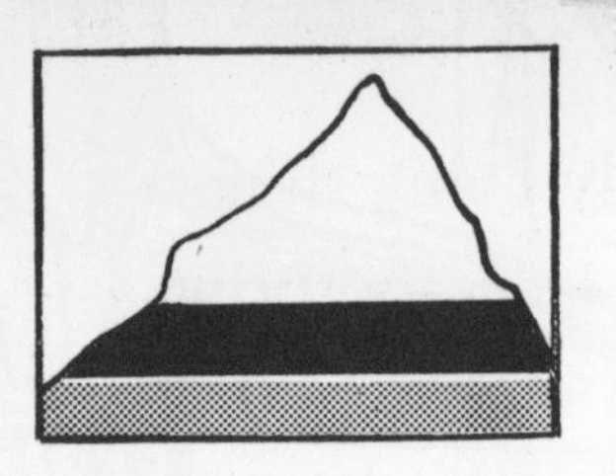

Now the trail turns sharply upward. This part of the mountain is quite different from the foothills.

We still feel hot in the sun, but the trees grow closer together. They are bigger and taller than the trees down below. Spreading black oaks, enormous yellow pines, graceful cedars, firs that look like Christmas trees—we see them all around us.

Wherever the trees don't shut out all the light, flowers are growing. White, blue, yellow, red—they make a wild garden in the forest. At our feet blooms a mariposa lily, its waxy petals open wide to the sun.

While we've been looking at the plants, animals have been busy all around us. Squawk, squawk! Down from the pine comes a jay. Off he goes to look for acorns. And there are plenty of them. But the jay is not the only acorn hunter. A fat gray squirrel is looking for acorns, too. Now he's found one. He holds it in his front paws, but he's not going to eat it right away. He finds a soft spot in the dirt and buries it. Maybe he'll find it again when he's hungry. If he doesn't, perhaps the acorn will grow into an oak tree.

Ahead of us, a little stream rushes down the mountain. The water is white and foamy on the rocks, brownish green in the pools. We wade through knee-high ferns and our feet sink into moss along the bank. What a change from the hot, dry slopes lower down! We dabble our fingers in the water. It's cold! It must have come from high up the mountain where the snow is melting.

We look back at the creek. We can hardly believe our eyes. Is that bird *walking under water*? Out it pops onto a rock, where it dips its body up and down. In fact, it is named the dipper. Then it goes back to hunt for insects under water. Its big, strong feet keep it from slipping on the rocks. Its fluffy oily feathers keep it from getting wet and cold even in this chilly stream.

Up we go again. The air is cool and fresh. The trees are very tall. High above us their branches reach into the sunlight, but down here we walk in heavy shade. Our feet sink into spongy ground covered with bark and pine needles.

Among the pines and firs we see trees so big that we have to rub our eyes. These are the Sierra redwoods—the giants of the mountain. They are the biggest, oldest trees in the world. They grow only in California, though a close relative is found in central China.

Let's stop at the foot of this one. What a game of hide-and-seek we could play here! A dozen people could hide behind this enormous trunk. We look up and up some more. The *lowest* branch must be fifty feet above our heads. The top of the tree is a cloud of soft green. We search the ground for a cone. Here's one. It fits neatly into the palm of our hand. What a tiny cone for such a huge tree!

This tree was alive and growing when Columbus discovered America. It is much older than the oldest building in our country. Its thick, soft bark is no home for most of the insects that destroy so many other trees in the forest. In the bark is a chemical that is poisonous to nearly all insects. Even forest fires have not killed this giant. Look at this streak of black in its hollow center. A forest fire once burned here. Perhaps during some long-ago storm lightning struck the big tree. Luckily the fire was not hot enough to burn all the way through the redwood's thick trunk. And now the tree has grown around the scar.

We climb over a fallen fir tree. It must have blown down in a storm last winter. Its wood is still hard and firm. A few feet away we see what's left of another tree. It must have fallen a long time ago, because we can stick our hand right into the wood and crumble it between our fingers. Once a tree falls, it begins to decay. Over the years, thousands of insects, worms, and tiny microbes feed on the wood and change it into different chemicals that then become part of the soil. New plants use these chemicals for their growth. And so each forest tree that dies becomes food for new trees.

Look out! We stumbled and almost fell over a mound of soft dirt. All around us are lots of these little piles of earth shaped like a half circle. One of them moves. More dirt is being pushed up out of the ground. Beside the pile a tiny nose appears, then the brown head and front paws of a small animal. A pocket gopher is digging out his burrow. He takes one look at us—then backs into his burrow without even bothering to turn around.

Thousands of gophers burrow under the ground of the forest. Their digging plows up the soil and makes it soft. When water runs over this loosened-up soil, it sinks down deep. In this way, gophers help the mountain forest to live and grow. They help to make its soil a vast sponge that soaks up the water flowing down the mountains. In one year the gophers in the square mile around us will dig up over *seven tons* of earth—enough to fill two big dump trucks.

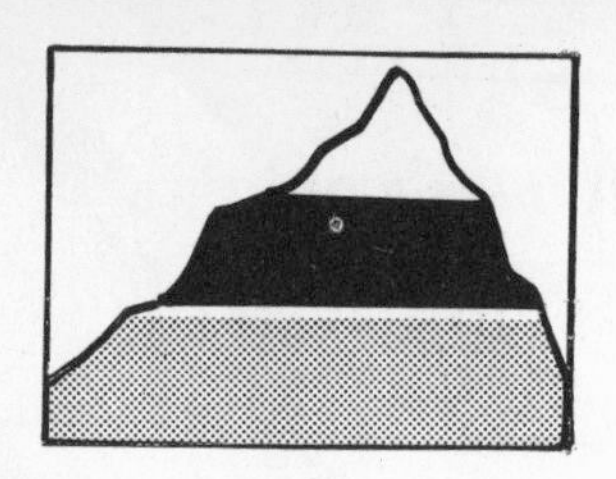

Again we move on to a new part of the mountain—higher and cooler. The trail zigzags back and forth toward a pass between two tall cliffs. We climb over sharp rocks. It's chilly in the shadow of the cliff. We stop to put on our sweaters.

In the distance we hear a sound like thunder. Is a storm blowing up? As we walk toward the pass, it gets louder and louder. We clamber around a point of rock, and there it is! A waterfall white in the sunshine.

Below the falls the water is pale green in a quiet pool. The rainbow trout are dark gray shadows against the rocky bottom. Low trees grow along the bank. Look at that willow. Its bark is all chewed around the bottom. A little mountain beaver must live here. We find the opening of its burrow in the bank, but we don't see the beaver. It won't come out until tonight.

We'd like to stay at the waterfall for hours, but we see the mountain peak far above us and we keep on walking. Flatter ground at last! The forest here is not so tall. The trail leads through a grove of lodgepole pines. As you can guess from their name, long ago the Indians used these trees to build their houses.

Crash! Out from the woods lumbers a big black bear. Two brown cubs follow her. The bear family looks us over. We'd like to pet the cubs, but we'd better not. The mother bear wouldn't like it, and we have a healthy respect for all two hundred and fifty pounds of her. Bears eat almost anything. This family has just broken open a wasps' nest and gobbled up the baby wasps. What will be next—nuts or berries or fish? Or fruit peel thrown away by a careless camper?

The bears are standing right in the middle of the trail. We walk slowly toward them. They turn and go about their business.

Fifty years ago fierce grizzly bears roamed this mountain. But people shot them one after another, until there are no more. Grizzlies are found now only in the wildest mountains of Canada, Alaska, and the Northwest.

Suddenly the trees come to an end, and we step out onto a mountain meadow. The thick green grass is dotted with the orange-red spikes of Indian paintbrush and the pale pink shooting stars that look just like their name. A cool breeze brushes our cheeks. The leaves on the aspens at the edge of the meadow flutter until the trees look as if they were hung with silver dollars. The late afternoon light is clear and golden.

This looks like a good place to camp. The grass on the lower meadow is damp, but we find a flat, dry place under the trees. We unroll our sleeping bags and start a campfire. Then we sit down at the edge of the meadow to watch.

Gray juncos with black heads bustle about on the ground, hunting for seeds and insects. Perky gray ground squirrels, with their short, skinny tails, give sharp whistles. They don't climb trees as other squirrels do. Meadow grass and seeds are supper for them.

Big holes and little holes! We see them all over the dry upper parts of the meadow. The small holes are the burrows of the ground squirrels. Up out of that big hole comes a squat furry animal. It is a badger. When it appears, the ground squirrels run. If the badgers did not feed on some of the ground squirrels, there might not be much of a meadow. Too many ground squirrels would eat up the green plants and leave it brown and bare.

That booming overhead is a male grouse. As the sun sets, he settles down on the branch of a pine tree. The mother grouse and her chicks wander about the meadow. When fall comes, the father grouse will leave them and go on up the mountain. Later in the year the rest of the family will move higher, too. Their thick feathers will keep them warm, and they will find good grouse food—treetops with seeds and pine needles sticking up through the snow.

The golden light is fading. Evening shadows cover the meadow. Only the peak of the mountain is still pale pink. Out from the edge of the forest come a deer and her fawn. Quietly we get up and walk toward them. They are not afraid of us. We can almost pat the fawn. We want to, but we don't. We won't disturb this happy family. Soon the mother and her fawn have eaten their fill of meadow grass. They walk slowly back into the forest.

Some animals live all year round on one part of the mountain. They stay in the spot where they can most easily find food and raise their babies. But deer are travelers. Every spring they start a trip up the mountain. As the snow melts and the leaves begin to grow, they work their way higher and higher. Then in the fall they travel down again to the lower parts of the mountain where deep snow does not cover up all their food.

Even the mountain peak is dark now. The air is biting cold. First we hang our food out of bears' reach. Then we crawl into our sleeping bags and look up at the stars shining between the branches. For a while we listen to the rustles, thumps, and squeaks. The meadow is still a busy place. Then we fall asleep.

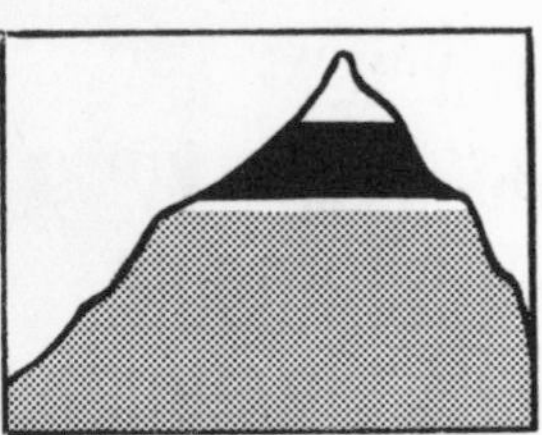

In the morning we're ready to start on the next part of the mountain. Now we're really going *up*. Our breath comes in short puffs. The air is thinner up here, and our bodies are not used to working with less oxygen. The early-morning cold is sharp, so we wear jackets over our sweaters. Every now and then a gust of wind swirls around us. The white peak of the mountain is closer now.

There are a few trees where we are walking, but they are not like the trees lower down. We touch the branches of a whitebark pine. Its twigs are so soft that we can really tie one into a knot. When the winter storms begin to blow, these trees will bend before the wind without breaking. The junipers are low and twisted. They, too, can stand the gales.

Kra-a, kra-a comes a harsh cry. A handsome gray-and-white nutcracker flies up from its nest in that juniper. It goes to work on a pine cone with its long, strong bill. First it uses its bill like a pick to open the cone, then it pries out the seeds. It gulps down one seed after another until the cone is bare. But the nutcracker does not live on seeds alone. In the spring it sometimes gets eggs from other birds' nests.

The nutcracker flies along beside us as we climb. The trail edges around the foot of a cliff. In the shadow is a white patch of snow. It never melts away, even in midsummer.

At first the rocks above us seem bare. Then we see small flowering plants whose long, thin roots hold them in cracks in the rock. They get their water from the melting snow. They are suited to life in this barren, rocky land, where only a few plants can grow.

What about animals? Surely they cannot live on these steep cliffs. But that rock above us just moved! It wasn't a rock at all, of course. Now we see it's a mountain sheep. It stands on a ledge against the sky—a beautiful animal from its long, curving horns to its tiny hoofs. Then away it dashes up the cliff, jumping from rock to rock. The mountain sheep's big horns help it to balance itself. It can get along well here on the mountain where it has few enemies. This shy animal, which leaps so gracefully among the heights, is nervous and awkward down on the flat land. The cliffs are its home. The mountain sheep here is very like its cousins who live much farther north in Canada and Alaska.

Something else is moving high above us. At first it is only a speck in the sky. Then it dives down—down—down. This is the biggest bird of the mountain, the golden eagle. Up it goes again. Its big claws hold a gopher. The eagle flies all over the mountain on strong wings. This one may have a nest far below us. The small animals of both the heights and the foothills are food for the eagle.

Ahead is a big rock slide. Granite boulders have come tumbling down the mountain from the peak above. The rocks are piled hit or miss, with little cracks and caves in between. If we sit very quietly, we may be able to see the animals that live here. Anyway, we're ready for a rest. We relax in the sun with our backs against a rock.

At first the rock slide seems empty. Then far off we hear yee-eek, yee-eek. Again we hear the same shrill whistle—this time closer. Several gray, furry animals are sitting on the rocks, looking around. They remind us of baby rabbits, except that their ears are round instead of long. They are conies. Another cony comes up the slope. It is dragging a big mouthful of green plants from the edge of a stream. One stalk is more than a foot long—much longer than the cony. It trails on the ground. The little animal carries its load into a crack between two rocks. We decide to take a look. There in the crack is a pile of green plants, like sweet-smelling hay in a farmer's barn. The cony is storing up food for the long winter.

Winter on the heights is no easy matter. We have already felt the bite of the wind even on this sunny summer day. Only a few weeks from now the snow will begin. It will pile up and up until the drifts are higher than a two-story house. Just as birds fly South in winter, some animals will go down to the lowlands where food is not so hard to get.

Up here the snow will cover both plants and the smaller animals. But some creatures stay here all year long. How do they live through the winter on these freezing heights?

The marmot is a very big squirrel. When cold weather comes, it hibernates in its burrow under a rock or a tree. For months it hardly breathes, its heart beats very slowly, it seems scarcely alive. In this deep sleep it spends the winter, while wild storms rage outside.

The little gophers who live on these heights have their own way of getting through the winter. They dig tunnels under the snow. There they find enough plants to keep them alive until late spring when the snow melts. Winter is a safe time for gophers, if they can find enough food. The deep snow hides them, and many of the larger animals and birds that feed on them have left the mountain.

But we do not want to wait until winter. The cold breeze reminds us to move on.

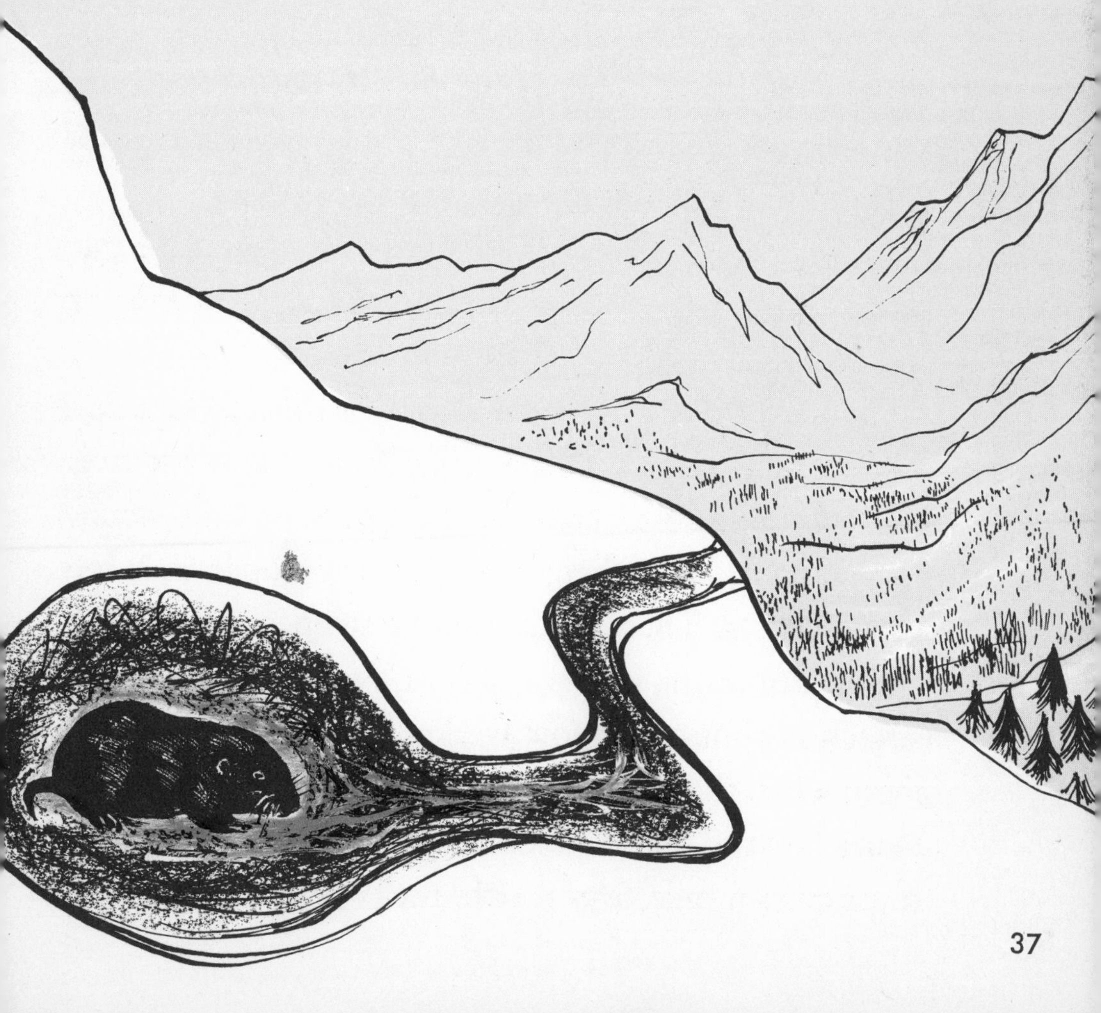

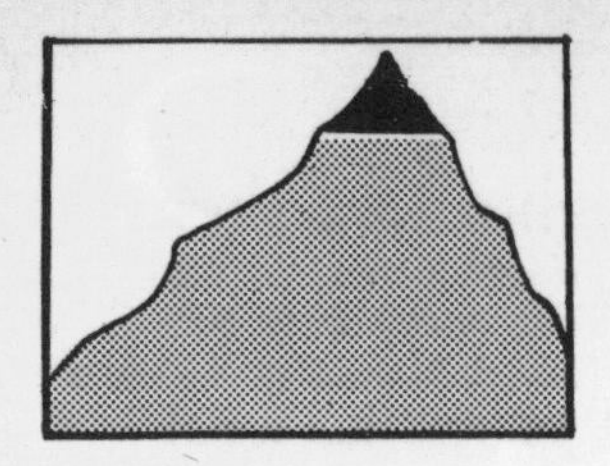

Timberline at last! No trees grow above here, and ahead of us the land is bare. On these high, rocky slopes there is nothing between us and the wind.

The sun is getting low in the sky. The peak of the mountain is gold, then pink, then purplish blue.

Time now to make camp again. We find a flat nook among the rocks near a small blue lake. The only wood we can find is a few scraps from the low bushes that grow in sheltered spots around the lake. But we manage to build a cheerful fire. Hot soup never tasted so good!

We take a last look at the stars before we snuggle into our sleeping bags. We're going to sleep in our tent up here—it's too cold and windy outside.

How much has happened since day before yesterday! In two short days we have gone from warm foothills, through tall forest, across bright meadows, and around rugged cliffs. First, there were the easy slopes with lots of flat places. Then the land grew steeper and steeper. Every turn in the trail was *up*. At every step we had to stretch our muscles. Now we know what mountaineers mean when they say that a mountain mile is a lot longer than a lowland mile. Our bodies had to work a lot harder to carry us a mile over rough, rocky trail.

In the morning we start off on the last push up to the top of the peak. Snow and rock, and then more snow and rock—that is all we see. The peak is like an island of never-ending winter, sticking up above the warm air down below.

Suddenly the wind blows in big gusts. We have to hang onto the rocks. Dark clouds cover the sun. Rain splashes in our faces. The thunder bangs. Is there any living thing up here besides ourselves? Impossible! Then we see them. Half-a-dozen small birds are flying right into the wind. A gust pushes them back, but up they come again.

The storm dies down. The birds fly over to the edge of that big snowbank and hop around. These are rosy finches, and they are finding their food right in the snow. The wind that pushed them around also brought them something to eat. The finches are picking up insects and seeds that the wind blew into the snowbank. There are no other birds up here to snatch away their dinner. They eat their fill—even on this cold mountaintop.

We climb and climb. Our legs hurt. Our cheeks burn with the wind. Our breath comes hard. We don't think about anything but the next step. Suddenly we stop. There are no more rocks in front of us. Beyond is only the open sky.

This is the top of the mountain.

We look down. What a change from the hot valley to this cold peak! And what a lot of smaller changes in between! Now we know what the colors of the mountain really mean.

The mountain is a big community made up of several smaller communities—the zones—piled one on top of the other. As we climbed the mountain, we found a new set of life conditions in each zone. The temperature, the amount of rain and wind, and the soil all changed. *We* were able to go through these changes by wearing sweaters and jackets and putting up a tent when it got too cold for sleeping bags in the open. But the other living things of the mountain have to stay where conditions are just right for *them*.

The quail of the warm, brown foothills cannot live above timberline and find food in the snow like the rosy finches of the peaks. The mountain sheep are only at home on the crags. The tall, straight trees of the green forests lower down on the mountain are replaced by the low, twisted trees that can bend before the wind without breaking. Even the flowers change—from the kinds that grow in the rich, moist soil of the forest to the types that can get water from mere cracks in the rocks.

Climbing a mountain is like wearing seven-league boots. Every time we went 1,000 *feet* up our mountain it was as though we traveled several hundred *miles* from south to north in the lowlands. In summer, the foothills where we started out are like the hot, dry country of northern Mexico. Yet on the peak, only a few thousand feet above, we stood in year-long cold like that of the snowy lands of northern Canada near the Arctic Circle.

Up here the animals and plants are more like those of the faraway north than they are like their warm-weather neighbors down at the bottom of the mountain. All over the world, plants and animals change as we go from a warm climate to a cold one. We can see these changes on the long journey from the lands near the Equator to the Arctic Circle. And we can also see the same kinds of changes mirrored in a shorter trip up a high mountain.

THE
END